ONCE UPON AN ARK

This book belongs to:

_____

ONCE UPON AN ARK

A Poem About Noah and The Lord's Animals

Written by Gail Patricia Cohen
For David who is the rainbow in my sky.

Illustrated by Christine Felicelli
*For my family and Frank; thanks for the
encouragement and support.*

Published by Roman, Inc., Roselle, Illinois

ONCE UPON AN ARK

A Poem About Noah and The Lord's Animals

Written by Gail Patricia Cohen   Illustrated by Christine Felicelli

Many, many years have passed,
since the fate of Earth was cast.
God decided He'd wash clean,
planet Earth from all He'd seen.

God picked Noah from the rest,
told him soon would come a test:
"Save my creatures, two by two;
This is what I ask of you."

Hammer, hammer night and day,
cutting cedars, loading hay.
Noah roofed the sturdy ark,
just as Earth was growing dark.

Clouds of thunder! See it crash!
Noah said, "We'd better dash."
"All God's creatures," Noah cried,
"let us now begin our ride."

Then God sent His promised rains,
into rivers, onto plains,
over forests and the bays.
Down it fell for 40 days!

In the ark, quite safe and dry,
all hands worked as time flew by.
Every animal had a job;
it was quite a funny mob!

Two plump chickens on their nest,
laying eggs for all the rest.
One made white eggs, one made brown,
Both taste yummy going down.

Since there were no garbage cans,
Noah had made other plans:
Garbage from the bow to keel
would provide a fine goat meal.

Elephant showers, watery spray,
bathed God's creatures every day.
Heavenly bubbles, rub-a-dub,
How we love to wash and scrub.

To watch over ark affairs,
Noah chose two big, brown bears.
Their reward? A honey treat,
gold and sweet, so good to eat!

Babysitting was a chore;
who had patience, books and more?
Which pair was both smart and sunny?
Noah's choice? The loving bunny.

"Patience, children," Noah preached,
"Learn from Tortoise how it's reached.
When the time has come to play,
let the monkeys show the way!"

Mighty lion, on this boat,
care for us while we're afloat;
Teach us to be brave and strong,
help us learn what's right and wrong.

Gentle goose, your feathers white,
make a bed for us tonight.
We'll rest in your tender care
following our goodnight prayer.

40 days! A thirsty crew
loved a drink from "Moo" and "Too."
They churned cheese and creamy butter,
From the dairy by the rudder.

Who will guide us through the night?
Who will be God's beacon light?
Which two can peek fore and aft?
Noah knows: two tall giraffe.

One day two doves flew away,
They found land that very day.
Both birds chirped, "The earth is green;
Let's tell Noah what we've seen!"

"Look! A rainbow points the way,"
Noah said this fine new day.
"Feel the sun, watch rivers flow.
Soon you'll see bright flowers grow."

As Noah promised, Earth grew dry.
Spring returned and all knew why.
God's lesson: "life" for all to see
Our Earth was saved . . . and so were we.

The Beginning.